THIS BOOK BELONGS TO:

CONTACT INFORMATION	
NAME:	
ADDRESS:	
PHONE:	

START / END DATES

_____ / _____ / _____   TO   _____ / _____ / _____

DEDICATION

This Petty Cash Book Journal Log is dedicated to all the people out there who record their petty cash and want to document their findings in the process.

You are my inspiration for producing books and I'm honored to be a part of keeping all of your petty cash notes and records organized.

This journal notebook will help you record your details about your petty cash.

Thoughtfully put together with these sections to record:

Previous Balance, Date, Description, Cash In, Cash Out, Float, Less Cash Left, Total & End Balance.

HOW TO USE THIS BOOK

The purpose of this book is to keep all of your Petty Cash notes all in one place. It will help keep you organized.

This Petty Cash Book Journal will allow you to accurately document every detail about your petty cash flow. It's a great way to chart your course through managing your petty cash.

Here are examples of the prompts for you to fill in and write about your experience in this book:

1. **Previous Balance** - Log the previous balance from the previous page or the previous book.

2. **Date** - Record the date of the transaction.

3. **Description** - Write the description of the transaction, whether it was a product or service, kind of payment, etc.

4. **Cash In** - Log amount in this column if it's cash in.

5. **Cash Out** - Record amount in this column if it's cash out.

6. **End Balance** - Write the end balance after the transaction.

7. **Float, Less Total Cash Left & Total** - Log the total end balance after the float and less cash left.

PETTY CASH LOG

DATE	FROM		TO		PREVIOUS BALANCE	

DATE	DESCRIPTION	CASH IN	CASH OUT	BALANCE
			TOTAL CASH LEFT	

FLOAT		LESS TOTAL CASH LEFT		TOTAL	

PETTY CASH LOG

DATE	FROM		TO		PREVIOUS BALANCE

DATE	DESCRIPTION	CASH IN	CASH OUT	BALANCE
			TOTAL CASH LEFT	

FLOAT		LESS TOTAL CASH LEFT		TOTAL	

PETTY CASH LOG

DATE	FROM		TO		PREVIOUS BALANCE	

DATE	DESCRIPTION	CASH IN	CASH OUT	BALANCE
			TOTAL CASH LEFT	

FLOAT		LESS TOTAL CASH LEFT		TOTAL	

PETTY CASH LOG

DATE	FROM		TO	PREVIOUS BALANCE

DATE	DESCRIPTION	CASH IN	CASH OUT	BALANCE
			TOTAL CASH LEFT	

FLOAT		LESS TOTAL CASH LEFT		TOTAL	

PETTY CASH LOG

DATE	FROM		TO		PREVIOUS BALANCE	

DATE	DESCRIPTION	CASH IN	CASH OUT	BALANCE
			TOTAL CASH LEFT	

FLOAT		LESS TOTAL CASH LEFT		TOTAL	

PETTY CASH LOG

DATE	FROM		TO	PREVIOUS BALANCE		

DATE	DESCRIPTION	CASH IN	CASH OUT	BALANCE
			TOTAL CASH LEFT	

FLOAT		LESS TOTAL CASH LEFT		TOTAL	

PETTY CASH LOG

DATE	FROM		TO		PREVIOUS BALANCE		
DATE	DESCRIPTION				CASH IN	CASH OUT	BALANCE
						TOTAL CASH LEFT	

FLOAT		LESS TOTAL CASH LEFT		TOTAL	

PETTY CASH LOG

DATE	FROM		TO	PREVIOUS BALANCE		

DATE	DESCRIPTION	CASH IN	CASH OUT	BALANCE
			TOTAL CASH LEFT	

FLOAT		LESS TOTAL CASH LEFT		TOTAL	

PETTY CASH LOG

DATE	FROM			TO		PREVIOUS BALANCE	

DATE	DESCRIPTION	CASH IN	CASH OUT	BALANCE
			TOTAL CASH LEFT	

FLOAT		LESS TOTAL CASH LEFT		TOTAL	

PETTY CASH LOG

DATE	FROM		TO		PREVIOUS BALANCE		

DATE	DESCRIPTION	CASH IN	CASH OUT	BALANCE
			TOTAL CASH LEFT	

FLOAT		LESS TOTAL CASH LEFT		TOTAL	

PETTY CASH LOG

DATE	FROM		TO		PREVIOUS BALANCE
DATE	DESCRIPTION		CASH IN	CASH OUT	BALANCE
				TOTAL CASH LEFT	

FLOAT		LESS TOTAL CASH LEFT		TOTAL	

PETTY CASH LOG

DATE	FROM		TO	PREVIOUS BALANCE

DATE	DESCRIPTION	CASH IN	CASH OUT	BALANCE
			TOTAL CASH LEFT	

FLOAT		LESS TOTAL CASH LEFT		TOTAL	

PETTY CASH LOG

DATE	FROM		TO		PREVIOUS BALANCE	

DATE	DESCRIPTION	CASH IN	CASH OUT	BALANCE
			TOTAL CASH LEFT	

FLOAT		LESS TOTAL CASH LEFT		TOTAL	

PETTY CASH LOG

DATE	FROM		TO		PREVIOUS BALANCE		

DATE	DESCRIPTION	CASH IN	CASH OUT	BALANCE
			TOTAL CASH LEFT	

FLOAT		LESS TOTAL CASH LEFT		TOTAL	

PETTY CASH LOG

DATE	FROM		TO		PREVIOUS BALANCE	

DATE	DESCRIPTION	CASH IN	CASH OUT	BALANCE
			TOTAL CASH LEFT	

FLOAT		LESS TOTAL CASH LEFT		TOTAL	

PETTY CASH LOG

DATE	FROM		TO		PREVIOUS BALANCE		

DATE	DESCRIPTION	CASH IN	CASH OUT	BALANCE
				TOTAL CASH LEFT

FLOAT		LESS TOTAL CASH LEFT		TOTAL	

PETTY CASH LOG

DATE	FROM		TO		PREVIOUS BALANCE

DATE	DESCRIPTION	CASH IN	CASH OUT	BALANCE
			TOTAL CASH LEFT	

FLOAT		LESS TOTAL CASH LEFT		TOTAL	

PETTY CASH LOG

DATE	FROM		TO	PREVIOUS BALANCE

DATE	DESCRIPTION	CASH IN	CASH OUT	BALANCE
			TOTAL CASH LEFT	

FLOAT	LESS TOTAL CASH LEFT	TOTAL

PETTY CASH LOG

DATE	FROM		TO		PREVIOUS BALANCE	

DATE	DESCRIPTION	CASH IN	CASH OUT	BALANCE
			TOTAL CASH LEFT	

FLOAT		LESS TOTAL CASH LEFT		TOTAL	

PETTY CASH LOG

DATE	FROM		TO		PREVIOUS BALANCE

DATE	DESCRIPTION	CASH IN	CASH OUT	BALANCE
			TOTAL CASH LEFT	

FLOAT		LESS TOTAL CASH LEFT		TOTAL	

PETTY CASH LOG

DATE	FROM			TO		PREVIOUS BALANCE	

DATE	DESCRIPTION	CASH IN	CASH OUT	BALANCE
			TOTAL CASH LEFT	

FLOAT		LESS TOTAL CASH LEFT		TOTAL	

PETTY CASH LOG

DATE	FROM		TO		PREVIOUS BALANCE

DATE	DESCRIPTION	CASH IN	CASH OUT	BALANCE
			TOTAL CASH LEFT	

FLOAT		LESS TOTAL CASH LEFT		TOTAL	

PETTY CASH LOG

DATE	FROM		TO		PREVIOUS BALANCE	

DATE	DESCRIPTION	CASH IN	CASH OUT	BALANCE
			TOTAL CASH LEFT	

FLOAT		LESS TOTAL CASH LEFT		TOTAL	

PETTY CASH LOG

DATE	FROM		TO	PREVIOUS BALANCE	

DATE	DESCRIPTION	CASH IN	CASH OUT	BALANCE
			TOTAL CASH LEFT	

FLOAT		LESS TOTAL CASH LEFT		TOTAL	

PETTY CASH LOG

DATE	FROM		TO		PREVIOUS BALANCE	

DATE	DESCRIPTION	CASH IN	CASH OUT	BALANCE
			TOTAL CASH LEFT	

FLOAT		LESS TOTAL CASH LEFT		TOTAL	

PETTY CASH LOG

DATE	FROM		TO		PREVIOUS BALANCE

DATE	DESCRIPTION	CASH IN	CASH OUT	BALANCE
			TOTAL CASH LEFT	

FLOAT		LESS TOTAL CASH LEFT		TOTAL	

PETTY CASH LOG

DATE	FROM		TO		PREVIOUS BALANCE	

DATE	DESCRIPTION	CASH IN	CASH OUT	BALANCE
		TOTAL CASH LEFT		

FLOAT		LESS TOTAL CASH LEFT		TOTAL	

PETTY CASH LOG

DATE	FROM		TO	PREVIOUS BALANCE

DATE	DESCRIPTION	CASH IN	CASH OUT	BALANCE
		TOTAL CASH LEFT		

FLOAT		LESS TOTAL CASH LEFT		TOTAL	

PETTY CASH LOG

DATE	FROM		TO		PREVIOUS BALANCE	

DATE	DESCRIPTION	CASH IN	CASH OUT	BALANCE
			TOTAL CASH LEFT	

FLOAT		LESS TOTAL CASH LEFT		TOTAL	

PETTY CASH LOG

DATE	FROM		TO		PREVIOUS BALANCE	

DATE	DESCRIPTION	CASH IN	CASH OUT	BALANCE
			TOTAL CASH LEFT	

FLOAT		LESS TOTAL CASH LEFT		TOTAL	

PETTY CASH LOG

DATE	FROM			TO		PREVIOUS BALANCE	

DATE	DESCRIPTION	CASH IN	CASH OUT	BALANCE
		TOTAL CASH LEFT		

FLOAT		LESS TOTAL CASH LEFT		TOTAL	

PETTY CASH LOG

DATE	FROM		TO	PREVIOUS BALANCE

DATE	DESCRIPTION	CASH IN	CASH OUT	BALANCE
			TOTAL CASH LEFT	

FLOAT	LESS TOTAL CASH LEFT	TOTAL

PETTY CASH LOG

DATE	FROM		TO		PREVIOUS BALANCE	

DATE	DESCRIPTION	CASH IN	CASH OUT	BALANCE
			TOTAL CASH LEFT	

FLOAT		LESS TOTAL CASH LEFT		TOTAL	

PETTY CASH LOG

DATE	FROM		TO	PREVIOUS BALANCE

DATE	DESCRIPTION	CASH IN	CASH OUT	BALANCE
			TOTAL CASH LEFT	

FLOAT		LESS TOTAL CASH LEFT		TOTAL	

PETTY CASH LOG

DATE	FROM		TO		PREVIOUS BALANCE	

DATE	DESCRIPTION	CASH IN	CASH OUT	BALANCE
			TOTAL CASH LEFT	

FLOAT		LESS TOTAL CASH LEFT		TOTAL	

PETTY CASH LOG

DATE	FROM		TO		PREVIOUS BALANCE		

DATE	DESCRIPTION	CASH IN	CASH OUT	BALANCE
			TOTAL CASH LEFT	

FLOAT		LESS TOTAL CASH LEFT		TOTAL	

PETTY CASH LOG

DATE	FROM		TO		PREVIOUS BALANCE	

DATE	DESCRIPTION	CASH IN	CASH OUT	BALANCE
			TOTAL CASH LEFT	

FLOAT		LESS TOTAL CASH LEFT		TOTAL	

PETTY CASH LOG

DATE	FROM		TO	PREVIOUS BALANCE

DATE	DESCRIPTION	CASH IN	CASH OUT	BALANCE
			TOTAL CASH LEFT	

FLOAT		LESS TOTAL CASH LEFT		TOTAL	

PETTY CASH LOG

DATE	FROM		TO		PREVIOUS BALANCE	

DATE	DESCRIPTION	CASH IN	CASH OUT	BALANCE
			TOTAL CASH LEFT	

FLOAT		LESS TOTAL CASH LEFT		TOTAL	

PETTY CASH LOG

DATE	FROM		TO		PREVIOUS BALANCE		

DATE	DESCRIPTION	CASH IN	CASH OUT	BALANCE
			TOTAL CASH LEFT	

FLOAT		LESS TOTAL CASH LEFT		TOTAL	

PETTY CASH LOG

DATE	FROM		TO		PREVIOUS BALANCE	

DATE	DESCRIPTION	CASH IN	CASH OUT	BALANCE
			TOTAL CASH LEFT	

FLOAT		LESS TOTAL CASH LEFT		TOTAL	

PETTY CASH LOG

DATE	FROM		TO		PREVIOUS BALANCE		

DATE	DESCRIPTION	CASH IN	CASH OUT	BALANCE
			TOTAL CASH LEFT	

FLOAT	LESS TOTAL CASH LEFT	TOTAL	

PETTY CASH LOG

DATE	FROM		TO		PREVIOUS BALANCE

DATE	DESCRIPTION	CASH IN	CASH OUT	BALANCE
			TOTAL CASH LEFT	

FLOAT		LESS TOTAL CASH LEFT		TOTAL	

PETTY CASH LOG

DATE	FROM		TO	PREVIOUS BALANCE

DATE	DESCRIPTION	CASH IN	CASH OUT	BALANCE
			TOTAL CASH LEFT	

FLOAT	LESS TOTAL CASH LEFT	TOTAL	

PETTY CASH LOG

DATE	FROM			TO		PREVIOUS BALANCE	

DATE	DESCRIPTION	CASH IN	CASH OUT	BALANCE
			TOTAL CASH LEFT	

FLOAT		LESS TOTAL CASH LEFT		TOTAL	

PETTY CASH LOG

DATE	FROM		TO	PREVIOUS BALANCE		

DATE	DESCRIPTION	CASH IN	CASH OUT	BALANCE
			TOTAL CASH LEFT	

FLOAT		LESS TOTAL CASH LEFT		TOTAL	

PETTY CASH LOG

DATE	FROM		TO		PREVIOUS BALANCE	

DATE	DESCRIPTION	CASH IN	CASH OUT	BALANCE
			TOTAL CASH LEFT	

FLOAT		LESS TOTAL CASH LEFT		TOTAL	

PETTY CASH LOG

DATE	FROM		TO		PREVIOUS BALANCE		

DATE	DESCRIPTION	CASH IN	CASH OUT	BALANCE
			TOTAL CASH LEFT	

FLOAT		LESS TOTAL CASH LEFT		TOTAL	

PETTY CASH LOG

DATE	FROM		TO		PREVIOUS BALANCE	

DATE	DESCRIPTION	CASH IN	CASH OUT	BALANCE
			TOTAL CASH LEFT	

FLOAT		LESS TOTAL CASH LEFT		TOTAL	

PETTY CASH LOG

DATE	FROM		TO	PREVIOUS BALANCE

DATE	DESCRIPTION	CASH IN	CASH OUT	BALANCE
			TOTAL CASH LEFT	

FLOAT		LESS TOTAL CASH LEFT		TOTAL	

PETTY CASH LOG

DATE	FROM		TO		PREVIOUS BALANCE	

DATE	DESCRIPTION	CASH IN	CASH OUT	BALANCE
			TOTAL CASH LEFT	

FLOAT		LESS TOTAL CASH LEFT		TOTAL	

PETTY CASH LOG

DATE	FROM		TO	PREVIOUS BALANCE

DATE	DESCRIPTION	CASH IN	CASH OUT	BALANCE
			TOTAL CASH LEFT	

FLOAT		LESS TOTAL CASH LEFT		TOTAL	

PETTY CASH LOG

DATE	FROM		TO		PREVIOUS BALANCE	

DATE	DESCRIPTION	CASH IN	CASH OUT	BALANCE
		TOTAL CASH LEFT		

FLOAT		LESS TOTAL CASH LEFT		TOTAL	

PETTY CASH LOG

DATE	FROM		TO		PREVIOUS BALANCE

DATE	DESCRIPTION	CASH IN	CASH OUT	BALANCE
			TOTAL CASH LEFT	

FLOAT		LESS TOTAL CASH LEFT		TOTAL	

PETTY CASH LOG

DATE	FROM		TO		PREVIOUS BALANCE	

DATE	DESCRIPTION	CASH IN	CASH OUT	BALANCE
			TOTAL CASH LEFT	

FLOAT		LESS TOTAL CASH LEFT		TOTAL	

PETTY CASH LOG

DATE	FROM		TO		PREVIOUS BALANCE		

DATE	DESCRIPTION	CASH IN	CASH OUT	BALANCE
			TOTAL CASH LEFT	

FLOAT		LESS TOTAL CASH LEFT		TOTAL	

PETTY CASH LOG

DATE	FROM		TO		PREVIOUS BALANCE	

DATE	DESCRIPTION	CASH IN	CASH OUT	BALANCE
			TOTAL CASH LEFT	

FLOAT		LESS TOTAL CASH LEFT		TOTAL	

PETTY CASH LOG

DATE	FROM		TO	PREVIOUS BALANCE

DATE	DESCRIPTION	CASH IN	CASH OUT	BALANCE
			TOTAL CASH LEFT	

FLOAT		LESS TOTAL CASH LEFT		TOTAL	

PETTY CASH LOG

DATE	FROM		TO		PREVIOUS BALANCE		

DATE	DESCRIPTION	CASH IN	CASH OUT	BALANCE
			TOTAL CASH LEFT	

FLOAT		LESS TOTAL CASH LEFT		TOTAL	

PETTY CASH LOG

DATE	FROM		TO	PREVIOUS BALANCE		

DATE	DESCRIPTION	CASH IN	CASH OUT	BALANCE
			TOTAL CASH LEFT	

FLOAT		LESS TOTAL CASH LEFT		TOTAL	

PETTY CASH LOG

DATE	FROM		TO		PREVIOUS BALANCE	

DATE	DESCRIPTION	CASH IN	CASH OUT	BALANCE
			TOTAL CASH LEFT	

FLOAT		LESS TOTAL CASH LEFT		TOTAL	

PETTY CASH LOG

DATE	FROM		TO		PREVIOUS BALANCE	

DATE	DESCRIPTION	CASH IN	CASH OUT	BALANCE
			TOTAL CASH LEFT	

FLOAT		LESS TOTAL CASH LEFT		TOTAL	

PETTY CASH LOG

DATE	FROM		TO		PREVIOUS BALANCE	

DATE	DESCRIPTION	CASH IN	CASH OUT	BALANCE
		TOTAL CASH LEFT		

FLOAT		LESS TOTAL CASH LEFT		TOTAL	

PETTY CASH LOG

DATE	FROM		TO	PREVIOUS BALANCE		

DATE	DESCRIPTION	CASH IN	CASH OUT	BALANCE
			TOTAL CASH LEFT	

FLOAT		LESS TOTAL CASH LEFT		TOTAL	

PETTY CASH LOG

DATE	FROM		TO		PREVIOUS BALANCE	

DATE	DESCRIPTION	CASH IN	CASH OUT	BALANCE
			TOTAL CASH LEFT	

FLOAT		LESS TOTAL CASH LEFT		TOTAL	

PETTY CASH LOG

DATE	FROM		TO	PREVIOUS BALANCE

DATE	DESCRIPTION	CASH IN	CASH OUT	BALANCE
			TOTAL CASH LEFT	

FLOAT		LESS TOTAL CASH LEFT		TOTAL	

PETTY CASH LOG

DATE	FROM		TO		PREVIOUS BALANCE		

DATE	DESCRIPTION	CASH IN	CASH OUT	BALANCE
		TOTAL CASH LEFT		

FLOAT		LESS TOTAL CASH LEFT		TOTAL	

PETTY CASH LOG

DATE	FROM		TO	PREVIOUS BALANCE

DATE	DESCRIPTION	CASH IN	CASH OUT	BALANCE
			TOTAL CASH LEFT	

FLOAT		LESS TOTAL CASH LEFT		TOTAL	

PETTY CASH LOG

DATE	FROM		TO		PREVIOUS BALANCE		

DATE	DESCRIPTION	CASH IN	CASH OUT	BALANCE
			TOTAL CASH LEFT	

FLOAT		LESS TOTAL CASH LEFT		TOTAL	

PETTY CASH LOG

DATE	FROM		TO		PREVIOUS BALANCE

DATE	DESCRIPTION	CASH IN	CASH OUT	BALANCE
			TOTAL CASH LEFT	

FLOAT		LESS TOTAL CASH LEFT		TOTAL	

PETTY CASH LOG

DATE	FROM			TO		PREVIOUS BALANCE	

DATE	DESCRIPTION	CASH IN	CASH OUT	BALANCE
			TOTAL CASH LEFT	

FLOAT		LESS TOTAL CASH LEFT		TOTAL	

PETTY CASH LOG

DATE	FROM		TO		PREVIOUS BALANCE

DATE	DESCRIPTION	CASH IN	CASH OUT	BALANCE
			TOTAL CASH LEFT	

FLOAT		LESS TOTAL CASH LEFT		TOTAL	

PETTY CASH LOG

DATE	FROM		TO		PREVIOUS BALANCE	

DATE	DESCRIPTION	CASH IN	CASH OUT	BALANCE
			TOTAL CASH LEFT	

FLOAT		LESS TOTAL CASH LEFT		TOTAL	

PETTY CASH LOG

DATE	FROM		TO		PREVIOUS BALANCE	

DATE	DESCRIPTION	CASH IN	CASH OUT	BALANCE
			TOTAL CASH LEFT	

FLOAT		LESS TOTAL CASH LEFT		TOTAL	

PETTY CASH LOG

DATE	FROM		TO		PREVIOUS BALANCE	

DATE	DESCRIPTION	CASH IN	CASH OUT	BALANCE
			TOTAL CASH LEFT	

FLOAT		LESS TOTAL CASH LEFT		TOTAL	

PETTY CASH LOG

DATE	FROM		TO	PREVIOUS BALANCE		

DATE	DESCRIPTION	CASH IN	CASH OUT	BALANCE
			TOTAL CASH LEFT	

FLOAT		LESS TOTAL CASH LEFT		TOTAL	

PETTY CASH LOG

DATE	FROM		TO		PREVIOUS BALANCE	

DATE	DESCRIPTION	CASH IN	CASH OUT	BALANCE
			TOTAL CASH LEFT	

FLOAT		LESS TOTAL CASH LEFT		TOTAL	

PETTY CASH LOG

DATE	FROM		TO		PREVIOUS BALANCE		

DATE	DESCRIPTION	CASH IN	CASH OUT	BALANCE
			TOTAL CASH LEFT	

FLOAT		LESS TOTAL CASH LEFT		TOTAL	

PETTY CASH LOG

DATE	FROM		TO		PREVIOUS BALANCE	

DATE	DESCRIPTION	CASH IN	CASH OUT	BALANCE
		TOTAL CASH LEFT		

FLOAT		LESS TOTAL CASH LEFT		TOTAL	

PETTY CASH LOG

DATE	FROM		TO		PREVIOUS BALANCE		

DATE	DESCRIPTION	CASH IN	CASH OUT	BALANCE
			TOTAL CASH LEFT	

FLOAT		LESS TOTAL CASH LEFT		TOTAL	

PETTY CASH LOG

DATE	FROM			TO		PREVIOUS BALANCE		

DATE	DESCRIPTION	CASH IN	CASH OUT	BALANCE
			TOTAL CASH LEFT	

FLOAT		LESS TOTAL CASH LEFT		TOTAL	

PETTY CASH LOG

DATE	FROM		TO	PREVIOUS BALANCE

DATE	DESCRIPTION	CASH IN	CASH OUT	BALANCE
			TOTAL CASH LEFT	

FLOAT		LESS TOTAL CASH LEFT		TOTAL	

PETTY CASH LOG

DATE	FROM		TO		PREVIOUS BALANCE	

DATE	DESCRIPTION	CASH IN	CASH OUT	BALANCE
				TOTAL CASH LEFT

FLOAT		LESS TOTAL CASH LEFT		TOTAL	

PETTY CASH LOG

DATE	FROM		TO		PREVIOUS BALANCE		

DATE	DESCRIPTION	CASH IN	CASH OUT	BALANCE
			TOTAL CASH LEFT	

FLOAT		LESS TOTAL CASH LEFT		TOTAL	

PETTY CASH LOG

DATE	FROM		TO		PREVIOUS BALANCE		

DATE	DESCRIPTION	CASH IN	CASH OUT	BALANCE
			TOTAL CASH LEFT	

FLOAT		LESS TOTAL CASH LEFT		TOTAL	

PETTY CASH LOG

DATE	FROM		TO	PREVIOUS BALANCE		

DATE	DESCRIPTION	CASH IN	CASH OUT	BALANCE
			TOTAL CASH LEFT	

FLOAT		LESS TOTAL CASH LEFT		TOTAL	

PETTY CASH LOG

DATE	FROM		TO		PREVIOUS BALANCE	

DATE	DESCRIPTION	CASH IN	CASH OUT	BALANCE
			TOTAL CASH LEFT	

FLOAT		LESS TOTAL CASH LEFT		TOTAL	

PETTY CASH LOG

DATE	FROM		TO	PREVIOUS BALANCE		

DATE	DESCRIPTION	CASH IN	CASH OUT	BALANCE
			TOTAL CASH LEFT	

FLOAT		LESS TOTAL CASH LEFT		TOTAL	

PETTY CASH LOG

DATE	FROM		TO		PREVIOUS BALANCE	

DATE	DESCRIPTION	CASH IN	CASH OUT	BALANCE
			TOTAL CASH LEFT	

FLOAT		LESS TOTAL CASH LEFT		TOTAL	

PETTY CASH LOG

DATE	FROM		TO	PREVIOUS BALANCE		

DATE	DESCRIPTION	CASH IN	CASH OUT	BALANCE
			TOTAL CASH LEFT	

FLOAT		LESS TOTAL CASH LEFT		TOTAL	

PETTY CASH LOG

DATE	FROM		TO		PREVIOUS BALANCE

DATE	DESCRIPTION	CASH IN	CASH OUT	BALANCE
			TOTAL CASH LEFT	

FLOAT		LESS TOTAL CASH LEFT		TOTAL	

PETTY CASH LOG

DATE	FROM		TO		PREVIOUS BALANCE		

DATE	DESCRIPTION	CASH IN	CASH OUT	BALANCE
			TOTAL CASH LEFT	

FLOAT		LESS TOTAL CASH LEFT		TOTAL	

PETTY CASH LOG

DATE	FROM		TO		PREVIOUS BALANCE	

DATE	DESCRIPTION	CASH IN	CASH OUT	BALANCE
			TOTAL CASH LEFT	

FLOAT		LESS TOTAL CASH LEFT		TOTAL	

PETTY CASH LOG

DATE	FROM		TO		PREVIOUS BALANCE

DATE	DESCRIPTION	CASH IN	CASH OUT	BALANCE
			TOTAL CASH LEFT	

FLOAT		LESS TOTAL CASH LEFT		TOTAL	

PETTY CASH LOG

DATE	FROM		TO		PREVIOUS BALANCE

DATE	DESCRIPTION	CASH IN	CASH OUT	BALANCE
			TOTAL CASH LEFT	

FLOAT		LESS TOTAL CASH LEFT		TOTAL	

PETTY CASH LOG

DATE	FROM		TO		PREVIOUS BALANCE		

DATE	DESCRIPTION	CASH IN	CASH OUT	BALANCE
			TOTAL CASH LEFT	

FLOAT		LESS TOTAL CASH LEFT		TOTAL	

PETTY CASH LOG

DATE	FROM		TO		PREVIOUS BALANCE	

DATE	DESCRIPTION	CASH IN	CASH OUT	BALANCE
		TOTAL CASH LEFT		

FLOAT		LESS TOTAL CASH LEFT		TOTAL	

PETTY CASH LOG

DATE	FROM		TO		PREVIOUS BALANCE		

DATE	DESCRIPTION	CASH IN	CASH OUT	BALANCE
		TOTAL CASH LEFT		

FLOAT		LESS TOTAL CASH LEFT		TOTAL	

PETTY CASH LOG

DATE	FROM		TO		PREVIOUS BALANCE		

DATE	DESCRIPTION	CASH IN	CASH OUT	BALANCE
			TOTAL CASH LEFT	

FLOAT		LESS TOTAL CASH LEFT		TOTAL	

www.ingramcontent.com/pod-product-compliance
Lightning Source LLC
Chambersburg PA
CBHW051759200326
41597CB00025B/4615